Undercover

Undercover

Wendy Morton

To Wendy,
for remembering —
Wendy Morton
June, 05

Ekstasis Editions

National Library of Canada Cataloguing in Publication Data

Morton, Wendy
   Undercover

   Poems.

   Poems.
   ISBN 1-894800-21-4

   I. Title.
   PS8576.O778U52 2003   C811'.6   C2003-911403-9
   PR9199.4.M66U52 2003

© 2003 Wendy Morton
Author photo: Jim Duggan
Cover art: detail from a painting by Michael Lewis

Published in 2003 by:
Ekstasis Editions Canada Ltd.   Ekstasis Editions
Box 8474, Main Postal Outlet   Box 571
Victoria, B.C. V8W 3S1   Banff, Alberta ToL oCo

THE CANADA COUNCIL | LE CONSEIL DES ARTS
FOR THE ARTS | DU CANADA
SINCE 1957 | DEPUIS 1957

BRITISH
COLUMBIA
ARTS COUNCIL
Supported by the Province of British Columbia

Undercover has been published with the assistance of grants from the Canada Council for the Arts and the Cultural Services Branch of British Columbia.

Contents

No, no, no, no! Come, let's away to prison:
We two alone will sing like birds i' the cage:
When thou dost ask me blessing I'll kneel down,
And ask of thee forgiveness: so we'll live,
And pray, and sing, and tell old tales, and laugh
At gilded butterflies, and hear poor rogues
Talk of court news. And we'll talk with them too,
Who loses and who wins, who's in, who's out,
And take upon's the mystery of things,
As if we were God's spies. And we'll wear out,
In a wall'd prison, pacts and sects of great ones
That ebb and flow by the moon.

William Shakespeare
King Lear

Undercover

CICADAS

with thanks to E.B. White

At eight in the morning
the cicadas sing.
They sing of the world: heat.
They sing of the morning: love.
They sing of the burning afternoon: death.

A summer cacophony of heat, love, death.

And one last song at moonrise:
life, they sing, life.

ADVICE

Walk everywhere with your arms out,
disarm a stranger with a great first line.
Line your drawers with new lavender,
know that lavender has the smell of dreams.
Find a cold dreaming place, an old blanket,
imagine Florida.
Translate Lorca,
fill your arms with lilies and bees.
Forget everything.
Remember.

MID-SUMMER

You dream your daughters
before they are born:
see them at the green edge of a lake.
Mid-summer.
Waterlilies.
A kingfisher splits the afternoon.

They make their way over stones,
balanced like dancers,
move into the shallows:
find frogs,
hold them in their hands for a moment,
set them free.
Small flowers of their laughter
bloom at the shore.

And so you dreamed your daughters;
caught them dancing
in the mind's mid-summer:
held them for a moment,
held them, set them free.

RECIPE

Mistrust no one who offers you
water from a well, a songbird's feather,
something that's been mended twice.
Always travel lighter than the heart.

Lorna Crozier, "Packing for the Future: Instructions"

Watch.
Watch the wild roses,
the rosehips,
the maples' new leaves,
the twinned spruce,
the gilded broom,
the elderberry's ruby bloom.
Mistrust no one who offers you

this pallet of light.   Listen.
Listen to the breathing night
and the mourning birds:
the wild canaries, the extravagant ravens,
the hawks on the wind
and the gulls crying
on the broken Strait: hear the clear
water from a well, a songbird's feather.

Sing.
Sing old songs into the silver fog,
songs of love and sunrise:
try some icy Gershwin,
a Bach cantata,
Verdi's La Traviata.
Wrap yourself in a woven cape;
something that's been mended twice.

And dance.
Dance anywhere:
a quick tarantella, a broken tango
in the middle of the road;
on a crowded sidewalk
find a stranger and waltz.
Watch, listen, sing and dance.
Always travel lighter than the heart.

WAIT A MINUTE

You want me to learn the tango
and I only know how to waltz?
You suggest compromise:
dance lessons on Wednesday nights.
(I imagine some goofy guy,
slick with Brylcreem,
smelling of Old Spice,
who is solicitous,
light on his feet.)

Forget it.

I just want to waltz.
You could be Fred,
wearing a top hat and tails.

I could be Ginger,
wearing a feathered dress.
We could waltz in the garden,
spilling feathers
into the rhubarb and chard.

We could decorate the apple trees,
surprise the ravens,
startle the cat.

Music

I can't give this language a name.
The sign says,
"the best in progressive house
and trance."

I know the words.
Progressive: the snail's iridescent trail
from kale to grass.
House: geraniums;
woodsmoke; the kitchen's clatter;
garlic roasting; old poems.

Trance: how the clouds shape the sky
with dark rain;
how the rain drums
on the singing Strait.

I want the best:
progress, house,
entrancement,
music.

Polka Lesson

The sign said, "Polka Bob, your polka or mine."
Bob was 17, playing
his sunny yellow accordion
for toonies in the park.

When his cell phone rang he answered, said,
"I can't talk now, there's a crowd."
Which was me, one grandmother,
and Kenny, at 13 months.
I grabbed Kenny's little hands,
moved with him to the polka beat
of Smoky Moke's honky Chicago cake walk,
until he got it,
began to move his feet in time.

His grandma clapped,
Kenny hung on
and suddenly we were dancing in the park,
learning the polka.

At the Crocodile Cafe

The regulars at the Crocodile Cafe
talk politics, hummingbirds.

They decide that politicians
fly blindly into lies:
birds make more sense, they say,
and the talk turns to purple martins,
indigo buntings,
and the ruby-throated hummingbird.

Now there's a bird that's got some sense, one says,
"Last year I had 32 perching
on my shoulders, arms and hands;
all waiting for the feeder to fill.
I was their bridge between the earth and sky."

The other said he planted
wild columbine, bee balm,
coral honeysuckle and phlox
to keep them all around.
And how they swam in the air
when he watered,
swept into the mist
like small swimming rainbows, singing.

Jewels, he said,
humming jewels. Rubies.

Prairie Lightning

The woman leans in the doorway,
watching the lightning break the prairie sky:
thinks nightingales, Chinese gardens;
lets her mind swing
against the prairie night.

She sees a white crane turning
in a curve of flight,
and suddenly, she is dressed in white,
her arms filled with cold jasmine;
a bride breathing patterns in the clouds.

She remembers that her life has been
a kind of singing with quiet birds;
she remembers her heart's bright music
and the dancing in blue moonlight
and the nightingales' small songs,
the lightning breaking the prairie night.

Familiar

The cat's spooked;
springs from his dreaming perch
on the couch to the floor in a mad line,
tail a fiery streak,
heads toward the door.

I think a hawk's
had a go at him
or he's seen a bear
crashing through the blackberries.

He's off his food,
sits all day on the back porch,
catching the raven trees
in his marble eyes.

He's my familiar.
I hold him close,
breathe in resin, salt, fog.
Cat, I say, cat, be safe.
Watch the blazing, perilous world.

LILACS

Lilacs
purple, white,
bloom this spring
even in rain, grief
fills the room with flowers.

BERNIE'S FUNERAL

Bernie left clear instructions,
money in the bank,
a letter from his lawyer,
detailed diagrams.

He wanted the Mormon Tabernacle Choir
to parachute onto the beach,
singing Beethoven's Ode to Joy.
When they were through,
he asked that his thin remains
be placed on a golden Viking ship,
with all his Mozart symphonies,
and a case of Dom Perignon;
Don Giovanni playing over the raging wind.
He asked to be launched into the singing Straight,
the ship set aflame with a burning arrow;
an exquisite sunset pyre.

His friends did the best they could:
found a wooden pallet down the road,
built a scarecrow out of a broom and wire,
draped Bernie's opera cape around it,
added his black beret,
photographs of his pals from Buffy's Pub
and a six pack of Molson Dry.

They set it all on fire with some kerosene.
The third wave put out the fire,
the fourth wave swept it clean.
And his friends sang and sang;
their voices rising over the Strait's cacophony,
in celebration
in celebration.

Holy Bones: September 11

Night.
In the broken cathedral,
the lights gild the ashen air;
turn gray dust to ochre.
Silent men in glistening masks
pass pails hand over hand.
The pails are filled with holy bones:
tibia, fibula, ilium, sacrum.

At the barricades,
past the crushed steel,
wait lovers, wives, brothers.
They hold lilies, roses, photographs;
cry out a litany of names:
Rasweiler,
Rustillo,
Woodall,
Andrucki,
Gambali.

And they weep,
their sorrow,
a broken benediction.

Something on the Wind

Amphibian, slick with decay;
I thought: otter, rat, feral cat;
hawk caught, dropped. Death.

I turned away.

My hands found the wild mint and thyme.
Then the sky turned dark
with forty turkey vultures;
they breathed the wind.
The air was thick with wings.
In a slow drift they circled, circled
the dead thing at waters' edge.

These are days of omens, portents,
the reading of stones.
We listen for the night heron laughing,
for the owl at the edge of the roof.
Watch for the weasel crossing the road,
or the coyote,
for ants swarming.

And fear circles and circles, silent as stone,
like vultures on the wind.

At That Very Moment

Nineteen children are blown apart
on a bus in West Jerusalem.
At that very moment
a woman is walking,
in a market in Paris, for instance,
falling in love with a man on skates,
who is playing Bach on the violin.
She imagines,
as she walks past
the whirling wooden stars from Thailand,
past the masks from Somalia,
that he will stop,
and break her heart into nineteen stars.
At that very moment
the children named
Ariel, Amir, Ilan, Orin, Raphael,
Raviv, Avfiva, Chaya, Ilana, Liora, Liat, Nava,
Shira, Zira, Shiri, Barak,
Gilad, Yakir, Shalom
(their names meaning: tree angel, rain jewel, life light,
beautiful song, spring splendor, precious joy, peace)
were blown into the stars.
At that very moment
she will know separation's jagged face;
fear's wooden mask.

Down Wind Fallout

They sailed downwind in boats
carved from breadfruit trees,
knew the refracted patterns of the waves;
could read the burning stars.
They found Pacific islands
of coral lagoons, coconut palms,
jasmine and mimosa.

They stayed.

And the green years passed.
Then the bombs arrived.

And children would dance
in the ashen wind,
in the fallout wind;
would call it snow.

And their children would lean into
the salt winds
that blew across their scarred islands
bringing cholera, cancer.

And no one would remember
how to read the silver waves
or how to read the brilliant stars.

This Was My Home

Mahmoud lives in a tent
on the rubble of his life.
This is my house.
This is my library:
my broken books.
This is my home.

The Israeli children
throw stones, jeer.
The Palestinian children
throw flaming bottles,
broken cement.

500 settlers,
2000 soldiers,
120,000 Palestinians.

The terrorist enters the restaurant,
lifts his shirt,
says, "Do you know what this is?"
13 dead,
80 wounded.

Mohmoud says,
this was an oasis,
there were date palms,
lemon groves, birds of paradise.
This was my home.

THE SCARF

You arrive wearing a ruby vest,
Venetian gold,
sorrow's ragged midnight coat.

I want to tell you about palm trees
and treachery.
Instead I talk of recipes,
of snow geese in January fields.

Later, I feed you green winter soup,
cornbread, blueberries.
I bring you an emerald silk scarf.
You wrap
it close around you,
cold and glowing
against the treacherous, golden world.

DROWNING

How she was radiant that summer,
on the island,
how she tended the asters,
the golden begonias,
the fragile, crimson roses;
how she wore dresses blazing
with hibiscus, plumeria, wild ginger;
how the hummingbirds came to her,
singing in their ruby throats.

How she was radiant that summer,
when she stepped into the Strait;
how the hibiscus, the plumeria, the wild ginger
floated around her;
how the hummingbirds sang,
thinking she was a garden.

WAITING FOR LAKE MICHIGAN

I tell the paint guy at Home Hardware
that I want a litre of Lake Michigan,
oil based, exterior, gloss.
He says the name is out of date;
that it will take some time to find it.
I am patient;
flip through the file of this year's names:
Barnswallow, Bitter Sea, Ferryboat, Paradise.
I am thinking of the man with winged despair,
who one sunny April afternoon
skydived from the 8th floor;
imagining himself a barnswallow over a bitter sea,
heading for the ferryboat to Paradise.
I could add some paint names to this year's list.
Promise,
Broken Promise,
Sorrow,
Lamentation,
Grief;
all glossy, exterior, permanent.

MONARCHS

She saw the scarf first:
a silk forest of Hermes twill,
and the monarchs: their orange wings
fringed in black, spread in delirious flight;
and she remembered the millions that froze
in the forests of Michoacan,
one bitter January night;
their wings a thick ice carpet of death.

Then she saw
the perfect shoes,
the creased slacks,
the crimson jacket.
A woman, hanging.

And she thought then
how this woman would miss
the crocus in bloom,
the sudden snowdrops,
and later, the carpet of magnolia
and plum blossoms, falling, falling.
How this woman would miss
the crescent moon sliding
between Saturn and Jupiter,
and the planets in cluster
like the monarchs
hanging in frozen clusters
in the green forests of Michoacan.

Birthday Greetings

You tell me on your birthday
your wife's best friend gave birth;
hours later, her mother died.

You can't understand so much joy
and grief in one day.

I tell you of the monks in Tibet,
who eviscerate the corpses,
with four long knife cuts in the morning sun,
then let the waiting vultures have their fill.

One monk crushes the bones,
mixes them with barley
for the vulture's last meal of the day.
Nothing's left.

The Buddhists call it sky burial:
the soul's shortcut to Nirvana.

There is no sense to things,
I tell you, nothing to understand;
only life's certain pain
and the vultures waiting
for the next soul
to carry on their wings.

WHAT LASTS?

The well preserved remains of a 550
year old man are to be cremated…thrown to the wind.
Robert Matas

Not the new moon in your mouth:
not songs
or the geometry of dreams.

In ice:
thorax,
spinal cord,
chest wall,
throat,
pollen from high alpine alder,
knives, sticks,
coats of fur.

What of the frozen heart,
locked in glacial ice?
Or the mind, the hands?

He lasted, this man in a woven hat;
perhaps a singer on the wind,
holding the blue moon
in his open mouth;
watching the starry geometry
of his frozen dreams.

PHOTOGRAPHS

I always knew if I were sad enough
I could just lie in one place for a while;
let the sun come in through the windows:
not that the sadness would go away—
just that I would be able to move again,
step by step:
do normal things
like make a lentil soup,
and stop saying the terrible words:
pancreatic, bronchial, metastases.

Friends (Photograph 1)

Someone took a picture
of our feet touching.

Later she soaked her feet in some
magenta potion sent by her brother
from North Dakota.

Years before we were so happy
for no particular reason,
once we danced together,
probably a little drunk.

I found her a husband,
told her, "invite him for dinner,
get him into the hot tub,
make a move on him."

She did, it worked.

On her 51st birthday
she threw up on the bathroom floor.

Later she called me up and said,
"Let's get all dolled up and go out for lunch."

When the last call came,
I sat by her bed,
listened to her breathe deep inside;
there was a kind of dark rustling—
I was waiting for her last breath;
thought something would fly out of her
and into me.

It did.

Kathleen.

(Photograph 2)

She could clean her house listening to old movies,
knew the dialogue by heart:
knew every song in *Oklahoma*.

She coughed that winter:
wanted to leave her husband,
the seaside house;
had packed up her movies,
her miniature roses.

She stopped calling.
One day her husband screamed at me
on the phone.

I knew her roses were dying.

I only got to see her once in hospice,
slotted into 10 terrible minutes.
She told me she had 3 new blue nightgowns,
tried to sing, "Oh, what a beautiful morning."

Shirley.

(Photograph 3)

She was a stranger at the Christmas fair,
selling gent's vests painted
with exuberant bosomed ladies,
fish with wings.

She told me she owned a purple wig.
I said, "give it to me."

She did.

Then she lost chunks of herself
in various operating rooms.

Later, she fell in love on the Internet,
went traveling with portable chemotherapy,
became inoperable.

She moved so quietly out of my life.

I remember her
sublime oceans…

Rooth.

Conversation on the 24th Floor

In your office there is high Toronto light,
your daughters' art,
small stone sculptures on a shelf,
projects piled on the floor, our words
that move across your desk like poems.

And a photograph of the artist, Joseph Beuys.
It heats the room.

You tell me of his *Zeige deine Wunde*,
an installation you saw years ago:
two gray mortuary tables
in a white room,
two metal scrapers,
their worn handles
wrapped in broken rags.

When you came near,
you told me,
there was the sound of weeping.

His face burns into your days,
reminds you of death's fiery call,
life's broken music.

PATRICIA OF NAPLES

for Patricia MacDonald

She died on via Leonardo Bianchi,
an unlikely Scot in the Ospedale Mondali,
Naples.

She imagined the nuns
were white doves,
singing to each other
in the high bright room,
where she lay, trying to breathe.

It was all right, she told herself:
she had walked down the via Medina
wearing her sequined dress and best gloves;
she'd had penne with gorgonzola,
stuffoli with strega;
drunk a brandy in the lobby of the Hotel Santa Lucia.

It was all right to die, she thought,
in the city of Saint Patricia of Naples,
who walked barefoot, her arms full of roses,
to the martyrs' tombs.

Everywhere she heard singing and music,
saw sequined lights in the city;
told herself that it was all right
to be in Naples, dying;
the smell of drying roses on the wind.

TALKING TO HIROSHIMA

I know about subduction zones;
in my one repeating dream,
plates shift,
pull apart.
I walk
in an abandoned landscape;
around me is mud, rubble,
terrible silence.

I was talking to Hiroshima
when I saw the sky
fill up with birds.
The windows rattled.
She said, "The earth is moving here."

She told me
she was lately in Japan.
When she was introduced,
people wept when they heard her name,
and she wept too,
for their burning memories.

That night I dreamt
my bones glowed:
I was burning, irradiated,
walking down a shifting broken road,
in Hiroshima, weeping.

CIRCUS MUSIC

It was the kind of night
when no one walks.
December and rain.
But Henry Bell walked.
Just at the moment the driver
turned toward her friend
who had touched her arm,
Henry fell into the night.
And all the circus music flooded in;
he saw them all:
the elegant midgets,
the bearded twins in cummerbunds,
the albino sisters,
the cowboy giants;
the legless, the turbaned, the flourishers.
All that was elephantine and circuitous
came singing to him
in the vertiginous dark.
Not death, not the beautiful acrobat hitting the ground,
not the knife thrower's assistant
with blood pouring from her heart.
It was the tattooed lady who arrived,
emblazoned with roses and tigers,
who took him out of the rain
and into the light;
held our her hand
and led him back onto life's giddy insistent wire.

Photo Album: Looking For Mother

I shuffle the photographs like a worn deck of cards.

1941: Winter.
My mother leans against the new Studebaker,
wearing mink.
Holds me.

1942: Summer.
Mother smiles on the porch stairs.
I'm on her lap, wearing tiny white shoes,
clapping.

1945: I am in the back yard, dirt on my face,
eating carrots, smiling.

1949: Mother is dressed in pearls and orchids.
I am bones, braids, buck teeth.

1953: Summer
I wear a skirt with apples,
Mother and I wear identical shoes,
like ballerinas.

1955:

1959:

1963: Winter
We wear pastel housecoats,
smiling, dressed in our best loneliness.

Then she disappears,
I look for her in the shadows
of the old photographs.
But I've missed her,
missed her sorrow and easy grace.
Missed her.

After the Living Let Me Go

After the living let me go,
the dead arrive
to hold on to me again.
They wait at the crumbling spa,
where they have taken the waters.
They are dressed in amber silk and tweed,
take tea at four o'clock,
stroll in the umber afternoon.
I want to hold out my arms to them
after the living let me go.

After the living let me go,
my grandfather, Victor, arrived,
wearing his Hungarian bowler, from 1912,
his arms filled with corned beef and Jewish rye,
asked me to go for a drive with him in his red Studebaker
to feed the ducks.
He could never pronounce my name,
called me "Vendula."
I could say his, "Grandpa"
after the living let me go.

After the living let me go,
my grandmother, Anna,
wearing diamonds and a blue apron
came into the room with a bowl of chicken soup;
showed me how to make pastry
and drink sherry at the same time.
We walked into the back garden,
picked cherries, made a pie.
She said my name,
after the living let me go.

After the living let me go,
my father, Robert, cold and impeccable,
passed by; took me for a stranger.
I showed him my poems,
old photographs, told him
how I sometimes spoke in his voice.
Then he saw his face in mine,
said he'd done too much in life to notice,
but he would wait with me a while,
after the living let me go.

At the Edge

I have sketched a portrait
of my unborn face:
it is unfinished, imagined,
shaped in the sand dreams
of my ancestors
or in the memory of sand.
A desert face,
caught in the Diaspora,
a wandering face.

Would I have wanted beauty for this
unborn face?
Would I have have softened the hard angles,
shaded the edges?

Would I have missed the mind's long grace,
its welcome pain?

Broken somewhere in the helix,
a tidal drift from sand to ocean,
to fog, to wind.
And so I live at the edge of the sea
in a house with worn blue steps.
I have grown used to the
green air of balsam, spruce and fir.
I have learned to stay at the edge,
to stay.

PEARLS

She said she was wearing pearls when the bear came and she fell down in the snow; said her ice pearls saved her. Her grandmother's pearls. My grandmother said "restring pearls every other year. Wear them in daylight, next to the skin. They'll become iridescent: blue, violet, rose and green. They are gods frozen tears; made from rain and lightning." These are the pearls of a Renaissance queen, a Belle Époque courtesan. These are the pearls from the blue green islands of Cubagua and Margarita. I wear my pearls in the snow, waiting for danger and sorrow. Lightning.

GREEN VELVET CHAIR

The artist understands that nothing stays the same:
that one day, while walking
in a field of Queen Anne's Lace,
he will remember the oak trees
that are no longer there,
and he will know
a certain heartbreak
for their lost beauty;
quite suddenly he will remember
the oak trees he climbed as a child;
the smell of bitter bark on his hands,
and how he played there,
swinging in green sunlight.

In Peel's "Venetian Bather" for instance:
how the bather is stopped
so quietly in play:
she does not know
the gilded mirror will break,
the elaborate tapestry will turn to dust:
and one day, while walking
in an empty field,
she will remember
when she was golden and lithe,
in a gilded mirror,
holding a white dress,
trimmed in lace;
she will remember the delicate silence,
the green velvet chair,
the fractured light.

WHY IS A RAVEN LIKE A WRITING DESK?
nearly a pantoum

The girl sitting cross-legged
on the highway island
at Blanshard and Finlayson
takes the toonie I toss her.

On the highway island
I see her before she sees me;
takes the toonie I toss her
shivering in the May wind.

I see her before she sees me.
She is dressed like the Mad Hatter
shivering in the May wind;
black top hat and magenta cravat.

She is dressed like the Mad Hatter,
she is pierced: eyebrow, lip, nose and ear,
black top hat, magenta cravat,
she glistens silver in the thin light.

She is pierced: eyebrow, lip, nose and ear.
When I roll the window down
she glistens silver in the thin light,
all smiles and mad delight.

When I roll the window down,
she asks me, "Why is a raven like a writing desk?"
all smiles and mad delight.
I try to answer the question the rest of the day.

She asks me, "Why is a raven like a writing desk?"
I imagine wings, singing.
I try to answer the question the rest of the day;
suddenly pierced silver, shivering.

49

Feral Parakeets: An Avian Geography

There are feral parakeets in New York City.
They perch on the ledges
of Barnes & Noble
on upper Broadway;
they are edgy literati:
canary winged, rose winged,
they fly like jungle poems.

Nearby in Queens
a solitary pigeon
knocks each night
on the door of the Burmese restaurant.
She is let in,
climbs the stairs,
is offered saffron rice and tea;
honoured, she sleeps.

In Desert Hot Springs,
at the New Hope 4 U Motel,
two chickens talk
in the shadows of the courtyard.
They are unlikely desert birds,
like the condo mourning doves
who prefer the heated pools
where they sing
in the make believe oasis.
Or the caged raven,
who cries and cries,
half mad in the terrible desert.

At home, the ravens
have found the compost pile;
when they fly into the high fir,
I can honour them and all that is wild,
feral, winged, flying in the green air.

Two Boots

Two empty boots outside
the Arbutus Cafe
rest at an odd fandango angle.
Muddied, split,
they won't make it to the Sally Ann.

A boozy, bootless guy
wanders shoeless down Jubilee Avenue,
doing a barefoot autumnal two-step.

He is nearly inextinguishable, jubilant;
dancing and dancing
into the burnished, halcyon afternoon.

BIG JOSH

Josh has a 1967 Shelby Mustang;
he's going to paint it navy blue
and shine the chrome until
he can see the whole sky
reflected in it:
the stars, the moon,
the northern lights.

He loves the inside of cars,
machines,
likes the way things work;
understands gears, ratios.

He's not big on words,
he's just big,
quiet,
thinking of engines.

SHERI-D GETS HER TABLE

She saw it in the window of the Sally Ann,
a poetry table painted parakeet green
varathaned so thick it mirrored her face.
She had to have it.

She figured she could carry it home,
lashed to her back with brilliant ribbons.
After the second long block
the wind came up; the flaps of the table
moved like wings;
for a moment she thought she'd fly.
Then the weight of it hit:
there was a flamenco dancer
on her back;
her mother,
with a pot full of butternut ravioli;
her parrot calling,
"want a kiss, baby?"
She didn't want a kiss,
she wanted to go home.
Which she finally did, delirious
and waited for her landlord to find her,
collapsed, outside her door,
still lashed to her flying table,
where she would someday write
her green and shining poems.

Spanking With Cabbage

My lunch companion
tells me there was nothing on tv the night before
but "Kink." She watched it.
She said the couple talked about
spanking, whips:
life on the kinky edge.
Then she turns to me,
whispers in a conspiratorial tone
that she's sure the couple behind us
were on the show.

I look. The woman's too blond, past fifty,
wearing a skinny string dress.
He's wearing a black leather bandanna;
an old pirate.

And they talked a lot about vegetables,
she tells me.
I imagine spanking with cabbage,
whipping with spinach,
tumbling with turnips,
bouncing with broad beans.

I give up,
order lunch:
Sicilian spinach, scalloped cabbage,
broad beans on the side;
living on the edge.

SHELDON'S A POEM

I know that before he speaks:
bald, shirtless, brown as summer,
he hands me a bowl of black cherries,
says, "Taste."

His fruit stand is a blue tarp
on an army Ford
he's named to honour his Uncle Mac,
who died, he tells me,
of a tumor in only three short weeks.
I buy a bag of cherries and a peach.

Then he reaches for his book,
asks me to sign:
shows me signatures from Taipei,
Yarmouth, Prairie Sunset.
I sign my name, then write,
"Blue Moon" with some delight,
so he'll remember I was at Yard Creek,
looking for a poem,
a story, a peach.

WHAT FELL FROM THE SKY

She was in the garden
when a skull fell from the sky.

She was about to pick the ruby mustard,
whose leaves reminded her of sunsets, wings,
when she saw the eagle's shadow
on the grass.
Suddenly, in front of her,
between the English peas and Yukon Golds,
was a skull smiling,
teeth intact.

She'd been putting her dreams
under the compost pile for years,
waiting for something to fall out of the sky.
This was good enough, she thought,
more delight than omen.

She took the skull,
filled it up with compost and dreams,
planted it with calendula and columbine,
hung it from the greenhouse
to catch the light and wind.

And so it lived again,
death's windchime;
flowers blooming from its eyes.

Bottles

*It takes more than money to make
something out of nothing.*
                    Tressa Prisbrey 1886-1988

When Wally Prisbrey died,
Tressa found his bottles
hidden in the eucalyptus trees,
under her satin wedding dress
in the attic,
in random, abandoned heaps
behind the garage.

He liked his vodka neat
and often;
was partial to Arizona Silver
and Celestial Ice.

She never knew when he was drunk,
only that he was dead
and she'd miss him drunk or sober.

So she took his bottles and some mortar
and built a bottle wall;
thought she could catch
his spirit in that way.
Then she built a bottle room,
brought in a piano,
transformed discarded sorrow
into lovely song.

And Tressa found that she could sing
in all that fractured light.
She'd finally found a voice that was her own;
high and bright as Arizona Silver,
cold and clear as Celestial Ice.

LUNCH WITH ELIZABETH

I choose Siam Restaurant
because I love the gilded Buddhas
that line the walls,
the smell of Thai chilies,
jasmine, tamarind.

Elizabeth doesn't talk
of cancer, chemotherapy, divorce.
We talk of someone who has lately died,
eat Pad Thai,
weep.
We could be friends.

In Thailand, in the ancient markets,
are garlic, shallots, watermelon
stacked to the roof.
For sale, on every corner:
sweet rice roasted in bamboo,
pineapple on sticks.
Anywhere you can buy a bird,
hold it in your hand
long enough to learn it's wingbeat,
then watch it fly,
return to where it's fed.

I could buy Elizabeth a bird in a box.
She could set it free.

Christmas Eve on Whiffen Spit

The Scotch broom is gold as spring,
the blackberries flower,
set green fruit.
Tufted ducks perch
on the rocks at low tide.

We walk midway down the Spit,
to a tree wrapped in wind twisted tinsel,
fishing lures,
one red Nike runner,
fish bones,
a stone on a rope,
a broken cup,
seagull feathers,
styrofoam.

At its base, gifts:
a painting framed in duct tape,
a driftwood manger
with one plastic sheep, a crab shell,
a starfish.

We bring our own gifts:
a wooden bird, without wings,
four lacquered apples that spell out "Hope,"
two tin hearts, to hang on the tree:
for the wind,
for the blackberry's December bloom.

At Lake's Edge

The old guy with one good arm
throws a stick into the lake
for his black lab.
He's brought a tape
of Viennese waltzes to pass the time.
The two sunbathers on the dock
with candy apple hair don't hear it.
We do.

We move onto the lake
in our silver boat.
You row to the lake's edge.
It's summer's hottest day.
The dragonflies land on us,
in exuberant conjunction,
tail to thorax;
we are enthralled.
We watch the jetstream of sandpipers
wash over us, land on the shore.
We see an eagle on his windfall island.
A goldeye dives.

We dive.
You ask me for a dance;
we waltz underwater,
conjoined at lake's edge.

Airport, Burning

We were somewhere between
Reward and Unity
on WestJet flight 41
when the attendant announced
the airport in Saskatoon was on fire.
We were silent,
imagined the worst:
a terrible prairie conflagration.
Then we heard an errant welder
had torched some drifting fiberglass.
We became euphoric, poetic
as we flew over Limrick,
Amazon, East Poplar
toward Manitoba,
over Flin Flon, over Dauphin,
into Winnipeg, the city of bicycles,
to wait for the next flight
to Saskatoon, the city of bridges, flames.

An Invitation For Happiness

At Pandora and Blanshard
a bubble machine works overtime
at the Backpackers Inn:
soap bubbles spill unexpectedly
into the blooming street.

I want an equinox celebration:
expect Fred Astaire
in tux and tie
to hoof it down the avenue,
singing "Puttin on the Ritz."

Instead three drunk guys
wearing bandannas and tie-dyes
are surrounded by soapy iridescence
and begin a slow incandescent shuffle
and dance and dance,
inviting happiness, spring.

Rust is Good Enough If It Glitters

The ladies of the dementia ward
love jewels of glass and plastic, even brass;
rust is good enough if it glitters.

They wear treasures from Value Village,
mix and match
cerise boas, Vernon Viper tee shirts,
sequined gowns, magenta kimonos,
crimson sweaters that read "A & K Trucks, try us,"
dusty cotton gloves.

When they look into the mirror
they can remember when the full moon was on them
and they could hold the moon in their hands
and they could sing in the salty moonlight
and they were beautiful,
and they were beautiful,
all salt and glittering rust.

QUICK TO THE HEART

Watching a poem in sign language

Her face is the poem's mirror.
Her hands become kayaks, parrots:
she gives shape to the air
with this singing calligraphy.
"Bear" is crossed arms.
"Fear" is a fist to the throat.
"Dream" is two fingers quick to the head.
"Peace" is a Tai Chi move.
"Pain" is quick to the heart.

I am Calling

I am calling you,
birds of memory:
birds the colour of sunflowers,
birds the colour of twilight,
birds the colour of storms and tears,
birds the colour of starfish and clamshell,
birds the colour of death and sunrise.
I am calling you.
I am calling.

Acknowledgements:

Some of these poems have appeared in the following magazines: *Canadian Literature, Room of One's Own* and *The Antigonish Review.* Other poems have appeared in the anthologies *Who Comes, Jean Paul?, Women of Glenairley, Moving Small Stones* and *Dinner Party.* They have also appeared in the chapbook, *An Invitation for Happiness,* published by Frog Hollow Press.

These poems owe much to the encouragement of my companion, Rod Punnett, and to the inspiration of Patrick Lane and Lorna Crozier, who have been my guides through the efflorescent forests of poetry.

I'd like to thank WestJet Airlines, who have allowed me to become the poet of the skies in celebration of literacy. I would also like to thank my publisher, Richard Olafson, for his open-hearted kindness.

Finally, I want to thank Russell Thornton, Allan Briesmaster, Jim Bertolino, Wallace McPhee, Robert Gore, Susan Stenson, Kuldip Gill, Pam Porter, Tanis MacDonald, Yvonne Blomer, Sue Gee and Isa Milman, those mellifluous poets, for their consistent and enthusiastic support.